M^{The}ontgomery Canal

and its Restoration

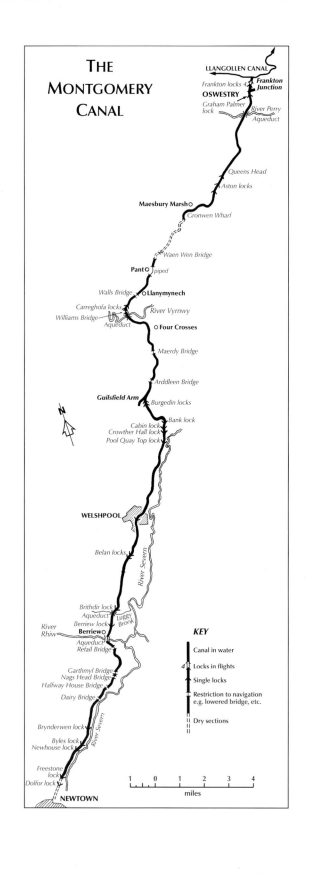

THE
MONTGOMERY
CANAL

LLANGOLLEN CANAL

Frankton locks 4 **Frankton Junction**

OSWESTRY

Graham Palmer lock

River Perry Aqueduct

Queens Head

Aston locks

Maesbury Marsh○

Gronwen Wharf

✕ *Waen Wen Bridge*

Pant○ *piped*

Walls Bridge ○**Llanymynech**

Carreghofa locks

Williams Bridge *River Vyrnwy*

Aqueduct

○ **Four Crosses**

Maerdy Bridge

Arddleen Bridge

Guilsfield Arm *Burgedin locks*

Bank lock

Cabin lock
Crowther Hall lock
Pool Quay Top lock

N

WELSHPOOL

Belan locks

River Severn

Brithdir lock
Aqueduct *Luggy Brook*
River *Berriew lock*
Rhiw **Berriew**○
Aqueduct
Refail Bridge

Garthmyl Bridge
Nags Head Bridge
Halfway House Bridge

Dairy Bridge

River Severn

Brynderwen lock

Byles lock
Newhouse lock

Freestone lock
Dolfor lock

NEWTOWN

KEY

— Canal in water

4▮ Locks in flights

▲ Single locks

╪ Restriction to navigation
e.g. lowered bridge, etc.

╏╏ Dry sections

1 0 1 2 3 4
miles

The Montgomery Canal

and its Restoration

Harry Arnold

TEMPUS

Dedicated to Jack Roberts, Shroppie flyboat skipper (left), and Graham Palmer, founder of the Waterway Recovery Group (right), friends and mentors who never wavered in their belief that the Montgomery Canal would be reopened. This is also dedicated to all the volunteers and others who have worked and are still working on the restoration of this canal.

Frontispiece: A map of the Montgomery Canal.

Front cover: Montgomery morning: Mist rises on the restored section of the canal at Queen's Head – now connected to the national network.

First published 2003

Tempus Publishing Limited
The Mill, Brimscombe Port,
Stroud, Gloucestershire, GL5 2QG
www.tempus publishing.com

© Harry Arnold, 2003

The right of Harry Arnold to be identified as the Author of this work has been asserted in accordance with the Copyrights, Designs and Patents Act 1988.

British Library Cataloguing in Publication Data.
A catalogue record for this book is available from the British Library.

ISBN 0 7524 1660 X

Typesetting and origination by Tempus Publishing Limited.
Printed in Great Britain by Midway Colour Print, Wiltshire.

Contents

Acknowledgements

A book on the Montgomery Canal was started as a joint project between Graham Palmer and I. Sadly, Graham did not live beyond the initial planning stage. I hope he would have approved of this final result. Much of what I know about this canal was told to me by boatman, Jack Roberts, who taught Eddie Frangleton and myself all about Shropshire Union history, boats and boating. Eddie, my oldest friend from schooldays, and I 'discovered' the derelict Frankton Locks together and have been Montgomery enthusiasts ever since. Much help also came from my friends, authors, artists and historians: Tony Lewery and Edward Paget-Tomlinson. Help also came from friends and acquaintances, past and present, in British Waterways, particularly Brian Haskins, Tony Condor and Sheila Doeg. Thanks for the loan of historic photographs, illustrations and items of information and other help to: Geoff Taylor, Mrs Nora Beech, Mrs Joan Rush, H.R.D. Lindop, Max Sinclair, John Horsley Denton, Mack Ozanne/*Shropshire Star*, National Railway Museum, A. & A. Peate Ltd, Hugh Potter and *Waterways World* magazine, Claud Millington, Margaret and Alan Clegg, Maurice Richards, J. Elwyn Davies, Dennis Hobson-Greenwood, Peter Starbuck, the Hyde family, Bill Thistlewaite, Sue and Mike Lambourne, Martin Grundy, Joseph Boughey, and for the map, Roy Davenport, and *Canal & Riverboat* magazine. All other photographs were taken by myself or are from my Waterway Images photographic library.

Last, but by far from least, to my wife Beryl, daughter Julie, and son Mike, for all their loving help and encouragement. See – I told you I would finish it!

The majority of the photographs in this book are from the Waterway Images Photographic Library specialising in all facets of rivers and canals: their history, traditions, craft, architecture and environment – past and present. For details, telephone 01283 790447 or 01538 361138. Visit the website at www.waterwayimages.com

Introduction

Leaving the Llangollen Canal at Frankton Junction, what is now known as the Montgomery Canal runs for thirty-five miles first to Welshpool then onward to Newtown. It starts in the county of Shropshire, crossing the border from England into the Welsh county of Powys. Although currently not navigable throughout, the line of the waterway remains complete almost to Newtown, with most of it in water. It is administered by British Waterways.

Like the Llangollen Canal, the Montgomery runs through some of the most spectacular scenery in the British Isles as it heads south westward into the Severn Valley and the border country of England and Wales, crossing the rivers Perry, Vyrnwy and Rhiw en route.

The Montgomery is a 'narrow' canal: its twenty-six locks are designed to take the 71ft 6in long by 6ft 10in beam of the horse-drawn narrowboat – unique to Britain's waterways. In canal engineering terms it is unusual in that it descends by twelve of these locks, from the Llangollen Canal towards the Severn, then climbs again along this river's valley via the other fourteen locks to Newtown.

Frankton Junction is just south of the village of Welsh Frankton, between Ellesmere and Oswestry. From here to the market town of Welshpool, the canal passes through the rural settlements of Queen's Head, Maesbury Marsh, and Pant. It crosses the border at Llanymynech, through Arddleen and Pool Quay, to Welshpool and on through Belan, Berriew, Garthmyl and Aberbechan, to Newtown.

Historically, today's Montgomery Canal was built by three different canal companies and the whole line took thirty years to complete. Like many of the rural waterways of Britain's 'canal era' it was a financial gamble, depending largely on local traffic, although the cheap transport it provided was responsible for the early rapid expansion of Newtown's woollen industry.

The Frankton to Carreghofa, near Llanymynech, section was opened in 1796, as a branch of the Ellesmere Canal. From here the Montgomeryshire Canal was projected and completed to Garthmyl, where it ran out of money in 1797. Financed by Newtown entrepreneur, William Pugh, a new Act of Parliament for the Montgomeryshire Canal, Western Branch, was obtained in 1815 and the line completed to Newtown in 1819.

Many famous waterway engineers were involved in its rather piecemeal planning and construction: William Jessop, Thomas Telford, John Dadford, Thomas Dadford Senior and Junior, Josias Jessop and John Williams.

Various amalgamations of the constituent parts brought it into the network of the Shropshire Union Railway & Canal Co. by 1850 and then under the control of the London & North Western Railway Co. (LNWR). In common with other waterways in the railway age, some decline followed and the Montgomery Canal passed into the hands of the London, Midland & Scottish Railway Co. in 1923. The LNWR had, however, encouraged traffic, such as their regular flyboat services, up to the First World War, as the canal gave them an entry into the territory of their rival, the Great Western Railway.

On 6 February 1936 the canal burst a few hundred yards below Frankton Locks. It was dammed off, no repairs were done and the LMS ignored their legal obligations. There was no national outcry, although local objections prevented official closure, but the fate of the Montgomery Canal was sealed. Legal abandonment came in 1944, with the infamous LMS Act of Parliament – obtained whilst the country was at war – which closed many miles of canal.

Under this Act road bridges were lowered, although none of the canal sold off. Under the 1948 Transport Act the Montgomery Canal passed into the ownership of British Waterways. It was classified as a Remainder waterway under the 1968 Transport Act, which meant that they could only undertake certain statutory work on the waterway. The last two miles into Newtown were sold off.

Volunteer restoration work was started by the Shropshire Union Canal Society (SUCS) in 1968 and led to the reopening of the length within Welshpool. This was followed by the restoration the section north of Welshpool to Burgedin, which was financed by one third of a million pounds raised by the Prince of Wales Committee. The country's first canal boat for the handicapped, *Heulwen/Sunshine* – initially funded by the ladies of the Inland Waterways Association (IWA) – began operating on this section. His Royal Highness, Prince Charles, The Prince of Wales, has taken a personal interest in the Montgomery project and has visited the canal no less than four times.

Left: William Pugh was responsible for many developments in the Newtown area, including turnpikes, a new Flannel Market, bringing gas to the town, starting a local newspaper and the completion of the canal by financing the Western Branch to the tune of £50,000. He never saw this returned, had to sell all his property to pay his debts and died in poverty in Caen, France, in 1842.

Opposite: Although there were long-distance traffics, such as the flyboat services and that to Peate's Mill, much Montgomery traffic was local. This boat in Lock 4 at Frankton appears to be carrying stone or coal. Bye trader Tom Moody with the boat *Endeavour* carried 20 tons of coal from Black Park Colliery, Chirk, to the Cymric Mill in Newtown every week until it closed in 1935.

Policies in favour of the canal's restoration were ordered to be included in the Shropshire and Powys County Structure Plans, by the Secretaries of State for England and Wales, in 1979 and 1980. Independent consultants reported on the cost benefits of restoration to the area and the nation: the first such report for any waterway scheme. Funding commitments from public agencies followed it, plus the promise of support from the European Community.

To legally facilitate restoration British Waterways obtained an Act of Parliament in 1987 – the first new Act for the reopening of a waterway. Arrangements were made with the Nature Conservancy Council to build off-line nature reserves to preserve the canal's important features of natural interest – again a first for the Montgomery Canal.

Despite all this support, an application to the Secretary of State for Wales to allow allocation of further public agency funds to complete a financial package for full restoration was turned down. If this had been allowed, over 50% of the package would have been recovered in grants from the EEC and the whole canal fully reopened. A 1988 House of Commons Select Committee recommended that the canal should be restored.

Within all the campaigning a significant step was the formation of the Montgomery Waterway Restoration Trust, as the major 'umbrella' organisation, drawing together and representing all the bodies involved in the future of the canal and to push the restoration forward. Sections have since been tackled individually by the raising of specific funding packages – often with the aid of local authorities and all amounting to millions of pounds – and by the application of direct, contractors' and volunteers' labour and skills.

SUCS volunteers moved on to Carreghofa and then on to Burgedin, restoring the two locks at each of these locations, whilst the IWA's Waterway Recovery Group (WRG) has restored the four locks at Frankton Junction and then the three locks below Queen's Head at Aston, including building a large nature reserve. Other major and important works have been undertaken by the staff of British Waterways throughout the length of the canal as part of their statutory maintenance duties or when engaged in a particular restoration project.

Dropped road bridges at both ends of Welshpool have been rebuilt, linking the town length with the section north through Burgedin to Ardleen and also allowing restoration southward through Belan and Berriew to Refail, thus creating the longest navigable section of the canal.

Following the restoration of Frankton Locks – and assisted by the bypassing of the original but filled-in A5 road bridge – the first four miles of the canal over Perry Moor to Queen's Head have been relined and reopened, including the building of a new aqueduct over the River Perry and a new bridge in the 'old A5' road. At the south end of the canal SUCS volunteers have rebuilt and reopened Brynderwen Lock.

A further funding package has enabled volunteers of WRG and the staff of British Waterways to extend navigation southward through Maesbury through Croft Mill Bridge. So part of the Montgomery Canal is once again connected to the national network and boats from throughout the waterways can reach Gronwen Wharf.

There are schemes and funding applications under preparation to extend restoration through to the Welsh border. Also, there are investigations into raising or bypassing dropped road bridges, which are still the main problem on the length within Wales, where SUCS has now started work on Newhouse Lock.

The Montgomery Canal will be reopened.

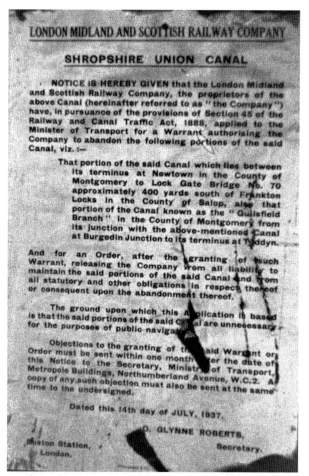

The official notice of closure under the 1944 LMS Act as posted in canal offices. This example survived for many years on the wall of the toll office at Ellesmere Port.

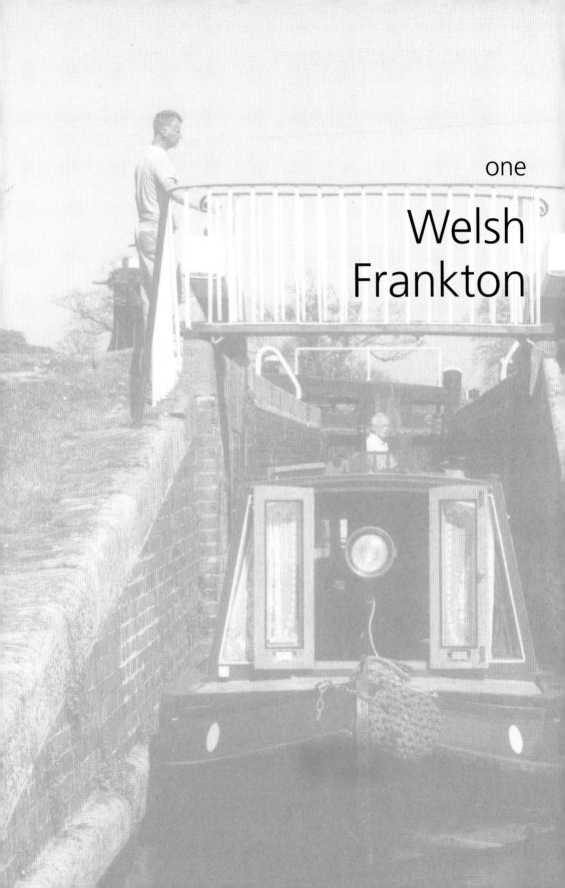

one

Welsh
Frankton

Above: Along with Welshpool, the four-lock flight at Welsh Frankton is the most photographed location on the Montgomery. This is the condition they were in when first photographed by the author on 7 September 1961: chambers overgrown, but still complete with gates, and some water still running through them.

Left: Some cosmetic work was done by the SUCS – such as the painting of the distinctive footbridge – but restoration didn't start until the IWA took responsibility for reopening the first four miles in September 1979. The iron towrope guard on the left spans the steps opposite the old Canal Tavern that were responsible for a number of people falling into the canal. Sam Owen of the Newtown flyboat *Trentham* was drowned at Frankton early one morning.

A Frankton Congregational Sunday School outing about to leave Frankton on a canal trip in 1921 in one of Hyde's boats: what the boatmen called 'scholar boating'. The Hyde family were boat owners, coal merchants, local transport operators and farmers and lived at the Canal Tavern. They still farm at Frankton and the old pub is their farmhouse.

The boatyard at Frankton was owned by William Jenks in 1851 and Henry Egerton up to March 1920. It was then bought by John Beech, who served his apprenticeship at the canal company's yard at Norbury Junction, and owned it until 1941. This view from the tail of Lock 3 is particularly interesting in that it shows the tight angle of entry into the dry dock, which was parallel to the line of the canal.

Viewed in the other direction from Lock 4, during the Beech family ownership, the wooden building on the right housed a power saw driven by a single-cylinder Petter diesel engine. The brick lock-keeper's cabin on the left, which sat on a solid slate slab over the bye-wash, was the home before the First World War of a man called Starkey, who was then in his eighties. He was charged 1s a year rent by the canal company.

Opposite above: The ex-Shropshire Union-carrying fleet boat *Aboukir* – which became part of the A. & A. Peate fleet – on the dock for repairs. Peate's were John Beech's main customer. He never built a new narrowboat but built skiffs and fishing punts, and also had a sideline in making coffins.

Opposite below: John and Nora Beech, their children and Nora's sister, Dorothy Harris, aboard the *Olga*: a 'change boat' – one owned by the boatbuilder and loaned out whilst a customer's boat was being docked. The bearded man in the centre is William Millard who did all the traditional 'rose & castle' painting and signwriting: Fred Hyde told me he 'turned a good rose'. Millard was also a visiting non-conformist preacher and there is a story of him preaching by the lockside and – in his fervour – falling into the lock.

15

One of the most famous boats in waterway history, Tom Rolt's *Cressy*. The acquisition of *Cressy* by the well-known author led to him writing the book *Narrow Boat* which was largely responsible for the formation of the Inland Waterways Association and the post-war revival of our waterways for pleasure cruising. *Cressy* was an ex-Shropshire Union fleet horse-drawn boat purchased by A. & A. Peate and

subsequently acquired by Tom Rolt's uncle, Kyrle Willans. She was converted for pleasure cruising in 1929-30 by Beech and a steam engine fitted. This remarkable and recently discovered picture shows her absolutely fresh off the dock before the steam engine was fitted.

Another unusual Beech conversion was the motorising of the Shropshire Union Railway & Canal Co.'s *Inspector* – built for management canal inspections – by extending the main cabin into an engine room and fitting a Chrysler petrol engine. The boat – owned by Mr Hobson-Greenwood and renamed *Hobsons Choice* – still retained the S-shaped knife, as on the bows of the early passenger packets, for cutting towlines of approaching craft and ensuring their undisputed right of passage. *Hobsons Choice* was broken up at Ellesmere shortly after the end of the Second World War.

Opposite above: In this Beech snapshot *Cressy* is afloat by the dock house and having the steam plant fitted. Rolt must have first seen her at this stage, when he spent weekends in Shropshire with his uncle, before the boat left for Trentham in March 1930. As a matter of historical interest in the life of such a famous boat, Rolt says in his autobiography, *Landscape with Machines*, that Kyrle Willans bought the boat from Peate's, but Nora Beech said that they first bought *Cressy* from Peate's as a change boat and then sold her on.

Opposite below: It is perhaps surprising how much pleasure boating went on in the 1920s and '30s. Beech also worked on another narrowboat conversion, the *African* for a Captain Carr Ellison, and built the cabin on this ship's lifeboat, which had the imposing name of *Sir Boris de Ganis*. Norah Beech is doing the painting.

Restoration work at Frankton was organised and undertaken by the IWA's Waterway Recovery Group (WRG) and involved visiting groups from other societies from all over Britain and sometimes volunteers from overseas. In this 'photo break' during work on Lock 3 on 21 July 1979 – emulating the formal navvies' pictures of old – are some of the then central figures in WRG including, in the back row, fifth from right, John Heap, the Chairman of the IWA, and eighth from right, Graham Palmer, founder of WRG. The main bricklaying team are mostly from the East Midlands group of WRG.

Work in progress on Lock 2: Hyde's farm (the old Canal Tavern) is on the right and the lock-keeper's house on the left. Watching the work are members of the IWA's 'four-mile restoration committee'. It should be remembered that any waterway restoration project probably involves just as many hours of committee meetings, lobbying and fund-raising as physical labour.

The first three lock chambers at Frankton are of brick construction and large areas of their facing walls were taken down and rebuilt. Lock 4 is a mixture of stone and brick patching, and volunteers are simply replacing the rotten brickwork on 21 February 1982. In a supposedly 'dry' canal, working conditions were often rather wet.

With the completion of masonry work on Lock 1, a Frankton 'first gating' ceremony was held on 10 October 1981 when a new top gate was officially lowered into place by Lord Biffen of Tanat, then the local MP, accompanied by Illtyd Harrington JP DL. A symbolic ceremony, as this is the gate that separates the Montgomery from the rest of the waterway network.

Other gates were not fitted throughout the Frankton flight until the summer of 1987, when the chambers were complete and ready for use. The gates were manufactured and fitted by British Waterways but paid for by the IWA as part of their commitment to the restoration.

Above: Frankton Locks were officially opened by
Dr Alan Robertson, Vice Chairman of the British
Waterways Board, on 12 September 1987, when a
procession of boats cruised down to the bottom lock.
Dr Robertson is standing in the forward cockpit of the
lead boat, with Ken Goodwin, then Chairman of the
IWA, sitting on the right.

Right: As many boats as feasible were allowed into the
lock flight, especially those of historical significance or
whose owners were involved with the canal. The ex-
Fellows, Morton & Clayton boat *Mendip* – from the
Boat Museum's collection – leaves Lock 3: probably the
first time a working motor narrowboat of this type had
ever used these locks.

23

After completion, the locks couldn't be used until the restoration of the first section of canal down to the River Perry. They were in effect ceremonially reopened again by the passage of the first official boat on 3 June 1995.

The staircase pair, kept immaculately by lock-keeper Colin Payne, and in regular use by boats making the trip down to Queen's Head and back to the Llangollen Canal in 1997. A remarkable renaissance from the dereliction in the same view on page 12.

two

Across
Perry Moor

Building the profile of the new canal bed below Lock 4 at Frankton in March 1994. Below Frankton Locks the canal crosses the flat river valley of the River Perry. Perry Moor is basically a bog, and most of this piece of waterway never had conventional lining because the canal water level was always on the level of the water table. Fine, until a pumping system was introduced after the canal was closed to lower the water table and improve the land for agriculture. Always referred to by the restorers as 'the dry section', this was the first really major problem in the reopening.

What became known as the Weston Arm goes off to the left before Lockgate Bridge. It was, of course, to be the main line to Shrewsbury before the final route of the Ellesmere Canal was decided. Lockmoor Cottage and this unusual single beam drawbridge once stood next to the narrows near the entrance to the arm.

Right: The dry bed of the arm near Hordley Wharf, ¾ mile from Frankton, on 11 November 1986. It breached near here in 1917. This remote area was called 'the wilderness' by the boatmen.

Below: Other wharves on the arm were Dandyford, Pedlar's Bridge and Shade Oak. The final wharf is here at Weston, on 11 November 1986, where the canal ended in a small basin next to this house and a warehouse, which Peate's leased in its latter days.

Above: This new spill weir, just above the Graham Palmer Lock, is on the site where the canal burst into a brook running into the River Perry in the early hours of 5 February 1936. In reporting it to the Chester office on 6 February, the local inspector attributed the cause to the bank being saturated by heavy rain and slipping on the peat beneath it. He ends his memo by saying, 'There is very little traffic on the section of Canal in question, and, as you are aware, it is under consideration by Headquarters to close it.'

Opposite: Correspondence regarding the possible repair of the breach went on for a year, with a final estimate of £600 being made for the reopening of the canal. This letter and the one on page 30 – from LMS file No.1/2452 (fortuitously rescued from burning by the author) – illustrate the attitude to the fate of the canal: finally confirmed by the 1944 LMS Act of Abandonment. Three boats are mentioned in the file as being trapped below the breach – Becks', Openshaw's and 'the company's boat' (presumably the *Berriew*). Some sort of temporary repair was made, allowing 2ft of water to be put into the canal, and the final letter of 17 February 1937 has a pencil note saying 'Openshaw's Boat moved from below Breach'.

(674
P W)

London Midland and Scottish Railway Company.

Memo FROM

THE ENGINEERING DEPARTMENT,

ELLESMERE

SALOP (Centre No.).

8th April, 1926

REFERENCE TO	IN YOUR REPLY PLEASE
YOUR LETTER.	EE. 22
	GIVE THIS REFERENCE.

To   R. E. Bullough, Esq.,

Chester.

Dear Sir,

Breach at Perry Moors.

A serious breach occurred in the offside embankment
of canal at Perry Moor situated between No. 70 Lockgate Bridge,
Frankton and Perry Aqueduct on the night of February 5th.

There is a watercourse at the foot of this slope and
the snow and frost caused the embankment to slip, which was the
cause of the breach.

This occurred between 10 p.m. on Wednesday February
5th and 7.30 a.m. Thursday February 6th, and approximately 5 miles
of water was run from the canal.

The stop planks were immediately fixed at No. 70
Lockgate Bridge and No. 72 Keeper's Bridge, and the length of canal
between Frankton Lower Lock and No. 1 Hordley Bridge, Weston Branch,
was refilled by running water from the top level through Frankton
Locks.

Between No. 72 Keeper's Bridge and Aston Top Lock a
good stream was running into canal which filled this level in a few
days.

It was then thought advisable to fix the stop planks
at Perry Aqueduct and remove those from Keeper's Bridge to allow a
further 7 furlongs of the canal to refill, as this would prevent
any cracks forming in the bed of canal and thus cause further
damage.

This length of canal has been kept normal by the
stream up to the present, but I do not think a sufficient supply
would be available during a dry period.

The length of canal now empty owing to the breach is
between No. 70 Lockgate Bridge and Perry Aqueduct, a distance of
approximately 1 mile.

Yours faithfully,

[signature]

E.R.O. 51563
OP. 3

LONDON MIDLAND AND SCOTTISH RAILWAY COMPANY.

ASHTON DAVIES,
Chief Commercial Manager.

T. W. ROYLE,
Chief Assistant Commercial Manager

T. E. ARGILE,
A. W. BARRETT, H. E. HORNE - PASSR.
C. N. MANSFIELD (Coal),
Assistant Chief Commercial Managers.

TELE phone—Museum 2900. Ext.....556
grams—"Davies, Euston, London."

CHIEF COMMERCIAL MANAGER'S OFFICE,

GP   EUSTON HOUSE, SEYMOUR STREET,

LONDON, N.W.1. 14th February 19 36

YOUR REFERENCE

IN YOUR REPLY PLEASE

D2/2107/P.

QUOTE THIS REFERENCE

Dear Mr. Massey,

> Breach in Canal Embankment near Frankton
> Junction.

Your note to hand this morning.

In regard to the estimated cost of actually re-building the bank, I have merely in the memorandum to Mr. Wallace stated that the subsidence is probably a little more extensive than was at first thought and that there is a possibility, I understand, of the rough provisional estimate of £400 being insufficient.

However, the point at the moment is that the Solicitor whom I have seen this morning, has approved a letter to the Minister of Transport telling him that the Company do not propose to proceed with the task of making this part of the Canal navigable and you will probably be hearing from Mr. Wallace in due course.

Yours faithfully,

C.H.Pemberton

F.W.Massey Esq.,
    Woodvale,
        Rothesay Road,
            Curzon Park,
                CHESTER.

The other letter from LMS file No.1/2452.

Two views showing a section of the bed dried out and virtually returned to agriculture. In September 1971 the IWA took the decision to be responsible for the restoration of the four miles from Frankton to the A5 road at Queen's Head, including Frankton Locks, with its Waterway Recovery Group heading up the work. A small WRG team, led by founder Graham Palmer, are making an initial survey of the canal's condition on 24 October 1971.

Above and below: Whilst volunteers worked on Frankton Locks, events overtook IWA as the scheme gathered momentum and – under the umbrella of Shropshire County Council – major grants became available for a first-phase restoration to the River Perry. It had been discovered that the canal had 'no bottom', because the old level had always been held up by the water table, so modern lining methods – a combination of butyl, concrete and gabions – had to used to re-create the channel during 1994.

With the second reopening of Frankton Locks, boats could again travel down to the River Perry from the main waterway network.

The drying out of Perry Moor had, however, caused a bigger problem in that – beyond the site of the breach – the whole bed had sunk. So a new lock with a drop of only about 75cm had to be built during 1994.

Opposite above: The death of Graham Palmer had come as a sad blow to the whole waterways world and the new lock was named after and dedicated to him. As he would have wanted, the dedication was a happy occasion, and some of his close friends and original co-founders of WRG unveiled a portrait stone in his memory by the lock on 3 June 1995. From left to right are: Mike Day, John Felix, the author and Colin Butler.

Opposite below: It would have appealed to Graham's wicked sense of humour that he has a 'little, awkward lock' named after him, which slows down the passage of boats.

Beyond the River Perry the next phase of the restoration work continued the reopening through to Queen's Head. This remote and straight section was built in 1822 to bypass a deviation forced upon the then canal committee by one of the original proprietors, William Mostyn Owen, so the canal would pass through his Woodhouse Estate, with an arm to his door.

Opposite above: Fortunately the original aqueduct over the River Perry was no great gem of canal engineering. It was in a ruinous state and the three tiny arches restricted the Perry's flow, when it was in flood, and were easily blocked by floating debris.

Opposite below: The old aqueduct was demolished and a new steel structure built – somewhat reflecting the 'Shropshire Union' style of earlier iron aqueducts.

Above: At the approach to Rednal is a small basin with a towpath swing bridge across the end – now a nature reserve – but which started life as a transhipment basin from the Chester & Shrewsbury Railway before railways into Wales were built. Transhipment probably finished around 1850-60.

Left: In 1858 the basin then became the site of Rednal Bone Works, seen here on 11 November 1986 before the building was demolished. Bone meal was brought by canal from various sites, including Ellesmere Port. Later owners, E.H. Richards, had one boat of their own, *Anita*, which carried sulphuric acid, first in bottles, then in fitted tanks. Boatmen had to lead their horses past the works because they were frightened by the smell.

three

Rednal and Queen's Head

REG^D 275 SALOP

SHROPSHIRE UNION

R · & · C · C^O

42

Perhaps one of most unusual buildings on the canal – seen here on 2 January 1976 – is the warehouse at Rednal Wharf. It was also where rail passengers, walking from the nearby Rednal & West Felton Station, boarded the passenger packet operated by the Wolverhampton Swift Packet Boat Co. for two years from 14 June 1852. The journey to Newtown, thirty-two miles and twenty-two locks, with a number of stops, took five hours and twelve minutes.

The Rednal warehouse was also used by the flyboat services and its immaculate restoration includes the original stop-board signals projecting by the roof. Skippers were fined 2s 6d for passing one of these signals set at 'stop'. They are seen in use on 17 September 2002 during a demonstration horse-drawn trip by the last surviving flyboat, *Saturn*, now being restored by the Shropshire Union Flyboat Restoration Society, in which the author is involved.

Queen's Head, looking back towards Rednal, on 13 August 1969, is where the canal crosses Telford's A5 road and, as the bridge had been culverted, was the first road obstacle to restoration.

Being sited on this main road, it was a major wharf and had quite a thriving industrial community, including Cotgreaves Corn Merchants Mill which closed in the 1940s. There was a sandpit on the other side of the minor road behind the warehouse and a still extant narrow tunnel under the road, through which trucks of sand were pulled to the boats by donkeys. A tragedy is recorded here when, in 1901, Julia Lyth, the daughter of the skipper of the boat *Caroline Mary*, was killed by a sack dropping off one of the cranes.

The solution to the A5 blockage lay in the building of the Oswestry Bypass in 1986, when this new bridge bypassed the original culverted structure, which then became part of a minor road.

This rather handsome new structure – carrying the minor road – was later built as part of the restoration project and opened on 21 September 1996, taking navigation through to the top of Aston Locks.

Above: Aston Locks – a flight of three chambers – lowers the canal down to the next long pound through Maesbury and Llanymynech. The house by the top lock (Lock 1) was originally the home and office of the toll clerk, who was also the lock-keeper, stableman and lengthsman.

Left: From Frankton the Waterway Recovery Group moved on to the restoration of Aston Locks. Here volunteers are working on the clearing out and rebuilding of the chamber walls of Lock 1 on 21 July 1988.

Opposite below: Like Frankton Locks, the restoration of the Aston flight was 'so good they opened it twice'. At the completion of work, WRG had their own reopening ceremony, using a workboat, in September 1998.

A 'problem' of the restoration scheme is maintaining a balance between boating use and possible damage to the rare and legally protected flora that has established itself in the waterway channel since closure. One of the ways this can be achieved is by the building of offline nature reserves. Concurrent with the restoration of the locks, during 1993, WRG volunteers built a large nature reserve on the offside of – and connected to – the canal. It was the biggest job to date ever undertaken by WRG and was funded by a national public appeal organised by the IWA plus various grants.

Although there was a trip boat operating on the then isolated section in Maesbury Marsh, below Aston, there was considerable work to be done on the channel before boats could be allowed down on to it. On completion of this work there was another official opening at Aston Top Lock, on 4 April 2003, by television personality John Craven, who is also a vice-president of The Waterways Trust.

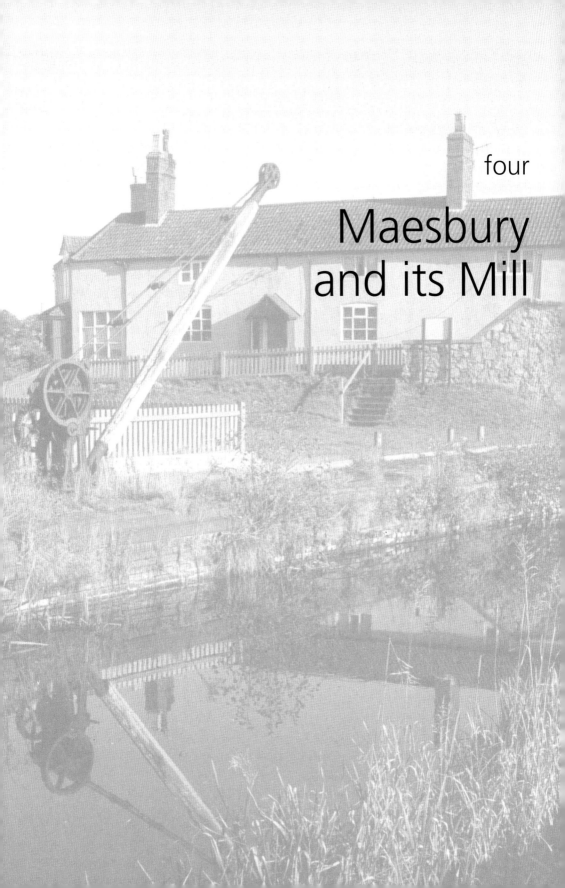

four

Maesbury
and its Mill

On 4 April 2003, after sixty-seven years, the village of Maesbury Marsh – and its Navigation Inn on the bridge – was once again connected to the national waterway network. The wharf was the main transhipment point for the town of Oswestry, and before the First World War the Shropshire Union warehouse had a two-horse dray and a staff of two porters and a drayman. One of the essential deliveries was Guinness. The warehouse stood behind the crane on the left and was destroyed by fire on 23 April 1968, while leased by Peate's.

Maesbury Marsh developed around the canal and has a number of imposing buildings which appear to date from the construction of the waterway. This is believed to have originally been the company agent's house.

Above: The *Inspector* – drawn by two horses – pauses for a photograph above what is believed to be the original Crofts Mill Lift Bridge. The imposing gentlemen aboard are probably officers of the Shropshire Union Railway & Canal Co. on an official inspection cruise. *Inspector* was recorded as being based at Ellesmere in 1934.

Right: Today there is a brand new steel Crofts Mill Lift Bridge – with safety features never seen on the original – sited next to the arm down to Maesbury Mill and a few hundred yards above Gronwen Wharf. This wharf was the terminus of the longest of a number of the canal's feeder tramways and is, in 2003, the present limit of through navigation from the Llangollen Canal.

Above: Maesbury Hall Mill stood at the end of an arm which runs alongside the Morda Brook. It was bought by the Peate family in 1862 and became probably the best-known business on the Montgomery Canal, if only for its fleet of narrowboats. The mill was finally destroyed by fire on 14 September 2002, a few months after the arm was again passed by a working narrowboat, on 4 April 2002.

Opposite: Canal traffic to and from Peate's Mill was initially via the boats of the Shropshire Union Railway & Canal Carrying Co. and some bye-traders until 1921 when the former ceased carrying. Peate's were keen to continue to use the canal as they had paid for the widening of the arm in 1913 and half the cost of dredging it in 1921. So they bought eleven of the redundant Shropshire Union fleet and later, a second-hand boat, *Lesley*, and had a new boat built, the *Margaret*: both were named after Peate children. This painting of the mill, from a 1920s calendar, is by Margaret Peate. The boats brought corn and maize from local wharves, on which Peate's leased some of the warehouses, and Canadian-produced grain from Ellesmere Port. Each boat generally did one round trip a week from Ellesmere Port, loading 20 tons of grain in 2cwt sacks. Boatmen earned about £3 a trip, or £5 with a return load. Return loads were generally road stone, sand, or timber. The state of the canal and the purchase of a lorry brought the end of grain-carrying in February 1934, with a final 420 tons moved by boat in the two months of that year. Peate's then sold the boats to other carriers on the main waterway network.

Above and below: The ex-Shropshire Union boats had stirring and historical names such as *Aboukir, Endeavour, Lemburg, Bethune, Sir John Jellicoe, Albania, Arcturus, Contraband, Manchuria* and the subsequently famous *Cressy*. The fully-loaded *Sir John Jellicoe* is seen above at Tower Wharf, Chester. There is also another unidentified Peate's boat on the dock in the background. Peate's virtually retained the Shropshire Union livery, substituting their own name and numbering in the panels. Also photographed below, just off the same dock, is *Bethune*. The large funnel is on a steam-powered barge!

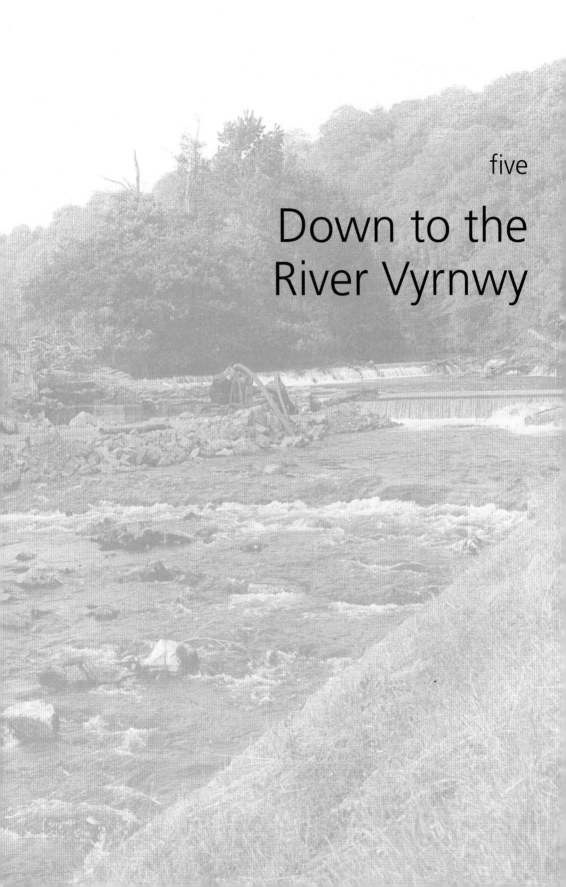

five

Down to the River Vyrnwy

From Gronwen Bridge the canal bed is currently virtually dry for almost three miles through to the south of Pant. The overgrown state of Crickheath Wharf in 1994 well illustrates this. This wharf was another tramway terminus.

Opposite above: Just to prove that the waterway in Pant once supported fish stocks, two canalside residents proudly display a large pike caught nearby; it is believed to be in 1932.

Opposite below: Although some surface water drains into the canal through Pant, the main flow is carried within a pipe laid under the bed, which will be a major problem in the restoration of this section of the canal.

55

Above and below: Little remains today of the canal and railway complex that was Pant Station, by the twin–arched Bridge 88. The smaller arch, by the offside wharf, carried another tramway from the Llanymynech quarry complex, which passed under the Cambrian Railway main line and also had a rail transhipment facility. By the time both pictures were taken, possibly in the 1920s, the tramway seems to be out of use. In the upper picture, what looks like a maintenance boat lies on the wharf and in the lower, the *Inspector* is again seen. Its two horses and their handler are waiting patiently on the towpath. This picture illustrates why the staff nicknamed the boat the 'White Elephant'.

The derelict state of the canal at Bridge 88 in 1994 is a startling contrast to the earlier views, although both arches of the bridge are in good repair. From this point – although not very deep – there is some water in the canal bed again.

On the offside, south of Bridge 88, before the Cambrian Railway crossed the canal, was Sam Owen's coal wharf. Although business was called S. Owen & Son, Sam had five daughters after whom his boat *Five Sisters* was named. *Five Sisters* is seen here at Frankton, fresh off Beech's dock after an overhaul and repainting. Owen was still using the canal in 1930.

Above: At Llanymynech the canal crosses into Wales. It is also crossed by the A483 trunk road, which remains in fairly close proximity all the way to Newtown and has created most of the major 'dropped bridge' obstacles to restoration. Llanymynech is a large village as it was once a centre of quarrying and in this 1970s view north from the bridge are the overgrown wharves, terraces and inclines of the Chubbs lime works, which processed stone brought down from the Earl of Powys's quarries on Llanymynech Hill. The chimney was that of a patent lime-burning kiln which operated continuously for twenty years up to 1914. Both the waterway and the site have been cleared and it is now the developing Llanymynech Heritage Area.

The River Tanat Weir – seen being repaired at a cost of £12,000 on 30 August 1970 – provides a head of water to feed this section of the canal at Carreghofa Locks. This breach in the weir threatened to cut off the water supply, after which sections of the canal could be sold off. The problem with the weir started the Shropshire Union Canal Society's campaign for the restoration of the canal and the subsequent reopenings.

Opposite below: South of the Llanymynech Bridge is what was the village's main wharf and winding hole, blocked by a large tree in 1997. The stable block on the towpath side is currently being restored and converted into an information centre and office. Just beyond this is an obstruction at Walls Bridge, where a piped causeway has been put across the navigation, but the bridge structure remains.

Restoration of the two Carreghofa Locks and the toll house was funded and undertaken by volunteers of the Shropshire Union Canal Society. Although they currently remain isolated they were completed, then officially opened by Lady White on 1 November 1986. The substantial lock-keeper's cottage was fortunately bought and renovated by a waterway enthusiast.

Opposite page: Carreghofa Top Lock in its derelict state on 13 August 1969. The present Tanat Feeder, dating from May 1822, comes in just above the top gate. Also, the official junction between the Ellesmere Canal and the Montgomeryshire Canal, Eastern Branch, which was at a somewhat nebulous but probably good legal dimension – '35 yards above top lock' – hence the requirement for the attractive toll house.

This page: Carreghofa Bottom Lock, in its pre-restoration state on 13 August 1969 and during the official reopening on 1 November 1986. Because of the jealous guarding of water supplies, the Tanat Feeder originally came in on the left, complicated by the fact that it flowed through a side-pond. When the original constituent canals were amalgamated the feeder was re-routed to come in above the top lock.

Opposite page: In 'political' terms, perhaps the most controversial bridge lowering was that of Williams Bridge – in progress here during 1980 – when the restoration scheme was well under way. The bridge was, however, in a very poor state for the traffic it now carried and would eventually have had to be replaced. This didn't stop the matter being brought to the attention of HRH Prince Charles, The Prince of Wales, who by this time had taken a personal interest in the restoration and was on his third visit to the Montgomery Canal on 11 July 1980.

Above: The canal's biggest structure is the Vyrnwy Aqueduct, seen here on 30 August 1970. Built in 1796 by contractors John Simpson and William Hazeldine at a cost of £4,500, it suffered from a collapsed arch not long after completion. Extensive repairs in 1823 by the canal's resident engineer George Watson Buck – who went on to do a lot of railway work – can be seen in the form of the iron cramps and strengthening struts. It has a long history of leakage and in 1971 British Waterways did considerable work on repairs to the channel lining.

Opposite: On the approach to the River Vyrnwy there are two sets of 'land arches' to allow for flooding of the valley. Unlike the main aqueduct, these are of engineering brick construction.

The inside of the Vyrnwy Aqueduct on 19 July 1971, when British Waterways had it drained for repairs.

At the south end of the Vyrnwy Aqueduct is a wharf, built in 1814 by Exuperius Pickering, which was a transhipment point for coal and other goods to be distributed by road westward into the heart of Wales. Just beyond this was another wharf with a very attractive building – the Pentreheylin Salt Warehouse (shown above) – built either in June 1824 or May 1831.

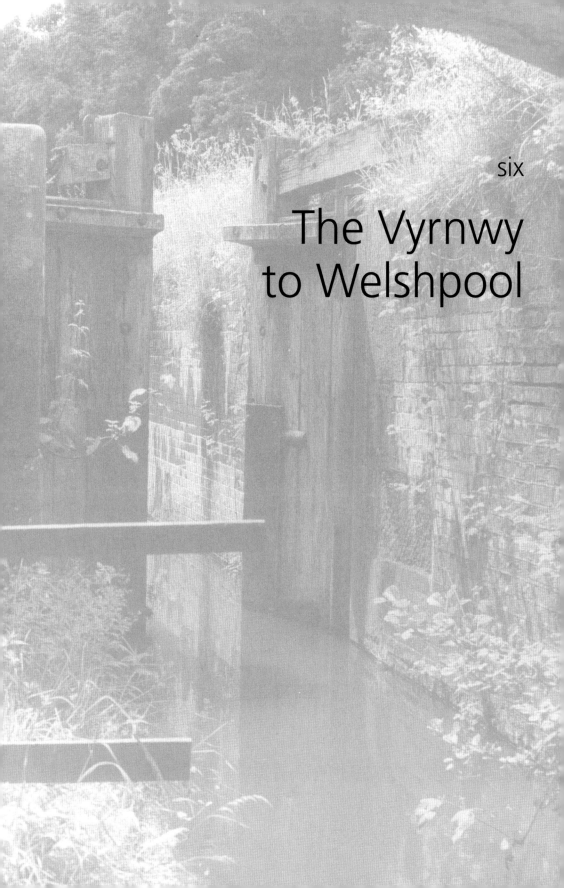

six

The Vyrnwy
to Welshpool

Left: At Canal House (or Clafton) Bridge, No.100, there were wharves on either side serving the adjacent village of Four Crosses. There were also lime kilns and a dry-dock, which there is no trace of now. On the north side was Clafton Wharf and on the south was this warehouse, built by Richard Goolden of Welshpool in 1836. In the flyboat service days, before the First World War, it was kept by Mrs Lloyd who had a famous swearing parrot that could also imitate boatmen's voices and used to tell their horses to 'gee up Charlie'.

Below: Probably the best illustration of a major dropped bridge on the A483 road is this one at Maerdy, which was flattened in 1949. Another one follows within a mile, built as part of a new section of road bypassing the village of Arddleen. Major plans to get around these two obstacles are currently (in 2003) being drawn up by British Waterways, in conjunction with road engineers and others involved in the restoration. Beyond Ardleen Bridge, No.103, the central, but isolated, restored and navigable section starts.

At the top of the two Burgedin Locks, seen here on 29 August 1969, the once navigable Guilsfield Branch goes off to the right. It is now a nature reserve. The lock house – much renovated and extended – is now British Waterways' main office for Wales.

Tyddin Basin, the terminus of the Guilsfield Branch, is one of the remote places on the waterway network and was once somewhat larger than in this 1969 picture. It had two warehouses and one of the surviving houses was once the Navigation Inn. One of the main cargoes shipped from it was timber.

Burgedin Locks were restored by volunteers of the Shropshire Union Canal Society, with funding raised by the society. The top lock is overgrown and derelict, but still gated in the above photograph of 29 August 1969. It was back in use for the official reopening (left) of the length to Ardleen Bridge by Welsh Assembly member Mick Bates on 2 November 2001.

Volunteers of an SUCS work party start to build the footings of a new concrete channel in the pound between the two Burgedin locks. It was required to prevent leakage.

The two locks were officially opened by the then British Waterway's Chief Executive, Dr Dave Fletcher CBE, accompanied by the then SUCS Chairman, Bob Johnstone, on 6 June 1998.

Winter on the lowest pound of the canal, which is just 1½ miles long. The surplus water, running downhill from both directions drains into the River Severn via a weir system that used to drive a mill at Red Bridge, No.106. An adjacent large clay pit, probably used in the construction of the canal, then used by a brick and tile works, has been turned into an off-line nature reserve. It is now generally called The Wern.

At Pool Quay the flight of four locks starts the canal's climb along the valley of the River Severn. It is difficult to imagine that the village was once the highest 'port' on the navigable river and an industrial site: 100-ton craft used to come up to a weir, which breached in 1881, and carried timber, lead and limestone back downstream. Traffic was taken over by the canal. Bank Lock, the bottom chamber, is seen above with vegetation cleared before restoration on 19 February 1976 and in use on 12 July 1992 (right).

Right: Although the four locks were derelict, all the operating gear was still in situ, and it was still possible to wind up a top gate paddle on 13 August 1969.

Below: The Pool Quay flight is very attractive and this boat descending the pound between Cabin and Bank Locks demonstrates how navigation and wildlife can successfully co-exist on the canal.

Restoration of the flight was undertaken under the auspices of the Prince of Wales Committee project funding and the work was done by volunteers of the Shropshire Union Canal Society and British Waterways staff. An SUCS volunteer points the walls of Pool Quay Top Lock on 19 February 1976 (above), and a boat passes through on 12 July 1992 (left).

One of the major restoration breakthroughs was the foundation of the Prince of Wales Committee by HRH Prince Charles to raise funds for specific projects in Wales. The Montgomery Canal was one and it was agreed on 25 October 1973 to restore the seven miles from Pool Quay to the dropped Gallowstree Bank Bridge, at a cost of £300,000, funded by the Variety Club of Great Britain. Dredging and bank protection work is in progress by the newly installed Abbey Lift Bridge on 19 February 1976. This section has become known as the 'Prince of Wales Length'.

There were two lift bridges on the length and the Moors Bridge is seen in its original wooden form in this postcard view.

HRH The Prince of Wales – then captain of the minesweeper *Bronington* – officially opened the restored length by demonstrating his skills in steering *Heulwen/Sunshine* through the replacement Moors Lift Bridge on 23 May 1976. Funds for this specially designed boat to carry children with specialist needs were raised by the ladies of the IWA.

How this length of canal north of Welshpool looked in its heyday, especially its immaculate towpath, is well illustrated by this postcard view, probably dating from the 1890s.

And after restoration in 1976, with *Heulwen/Sunshine* wending her way northward and the passengers enjoying the view over the Severn valley to the Breidden Hills.

seven

Welshpool

Blocking the link between the restored Prince of Wales Length and the reopened section in Welshpool was the dropped Gallowstree Bank Bridge, seen here as part of the original A483 route through the town. As the name implies, the local gallows used to stand near here, which may be why Dick Lewis, a skipper of the Welshpool flyboat, chose the spot to commit suicide.

A funding package was put together by county and local councils, grants and local donations and a new bridge – almost a short tunnel – was constructed using concrete box sections in October 1991. The main road through the town had by this time been bypassed.

The first boats, led by *Heulwen/Sunshine*, passed through the new Gallowstree Bank Bridge on the icy morning of 24 January 1992.

An official ceremony was held on 7 June 1992, when the bridge was formally opened by well-known actor and waterway enthusiast, David Suchet.

Above: There were a number of wharves serving industrial sites on the offside between Gallowstree and the Clerk's (Mill Lane) Bridge, including Powysland Mills. The iron boat *Joseph* – with the distinction of being engineering fleet No.1 – lies on Carters Coal Wharf and dry dock, *c.*1910. Until recently this site was the garage of W.R. Davies and excavations for a new housing development have uncovered remains of the dock and lime kilns.

Opposite: The view north from Severn Street bridge around 1900 shows a most peculiar boat and load lying on the wharf next to Farr's coach builders, above the aqueduct over the Lledan Brook. An iron crane serves the original Thomas Groom's warehouse opposite. Pleasure boating is already a popular summer pastime and the rowing boat was hired from coal merchant John Jones at 6*d* per hour.

Left: Winter brings another form of pleasure for the local Welshpool populace but also problems for canal traffic. The boat loaded with timber is firmly stuck in the ice. A new bridge for the Welshpool & Llanfair Light Railway now spans the waterway by the aqueduct, so this dates the picture as after its opening in 1903. The telephone has also arrived in the town.

Below: The Welshpool & Llanfair Light Railway officially closed on 31 October 1956 and Max Sinclair photographed the last special train, run for enthusiasts by the Stephenson Locomotive Society, crossing the canal on 3 November 1956. Fortunately the railway was acquired by enthusiasts in April 1963 and is now thriving, but was forced to terminate in the town at Raven Square. The last train passed over the bridge on 17 August 1963. No longer can we see the stirring sight of a steam locomotive crossing Welshpool's main street and the canal.

A particularly elegant iron and masonry aqueduct, dating from a rebuild of 1836 by J.A.S. Sword, spans the Lledan Brook. It also has an interesting weir and paddle arrangement, which once also fed a mill, that can top up, by-pass, or drain the canal. By 25 March 1973 the contrasting construction of the narrow gauge railway bridge just carried a footpath.

On the offside, immediately below Severn Street Bridge, was the wharf of the Welshpool Standard granite company, which was once linked by a tramway to quarries owned by the Earl of Powys. They owned two boats, the *Hilda* and the *George*. The latter, with its family crew aboard, lies on the wharf. Today the wharf is occupied by new flats (seen opposite).

In 1969 came a quite ludicrous proposal to build a new road, to bypass the A483, along the canal line through the town, which lay derelict and overgrown here on 13 August.

Opposite above: We know exactly when Severn Street Bridge was rebuilt as the year 1900 is recorded on a plaque dedicated to the Welshpool mayor of the time: Mr Howell who paid its cost of £1,304 7s 10d. Is he the imposing gentleman in the centre of the top row, being photographed with the men who did the job?

Opposite below: Severn Street Bridge, on completion, from the south side. More interestingly, there is a pair of the Shropshire Union's carrying fleet boats, unloading or loading, under the overhang of the warehouse and an engineering department boat moored in the winding hole. Flyboat services ran from Ellesmere Port to both Welshpool and Newtown; the latter being the longest run of all. However, for a period they suspended the Newtown service and transhipped goods at Welshpool into a specially built boat, the *Cambria*, which ran a fast shuttle service between the two towns

Above and opposite: Backing the campaign of the Welshpool Bypass Action Committee, the Shropshire Union Canal Society held a massive clean-up of much of the waterway through Welshpool over the weekend of 18/19 October. Nearly 300 volunteers – travelling from all over Britain, and assisted by local anglers and enthusiasts – turned out for each day of the 'Welshpool Weekend' Big Dig. Working with SUCS was the newly formed Waterway Recovery Group and the organisation was led by founder, Graham Palmer. To the amazement of the local population, by late Sunday afternoon, a boat was launched and the then Mayor of Welshpool, Councillor J. Elwyn Davies, cruised through the town.

The Shropshire Union Co. also had a smaller inspection boat, the manager's boat *Neptune*, seen at Weshpool Lock. It was built in Birmingham in 1900 as a 'canal overseer's' boat and is believed to have been used as a 'pleasure boat' from 1933 to 1942. Opposite the lock were the company depot, maintenance yard and local inspector's office; many of the buildings still exist. The inspector lived at the lock house. Timber, in the form of tree trunks, was loaded here and the boat *Manchuria* – later sold to Peate's – was sunk in the lock whilst doing this in 1910.

Opposite above: Unusually, a waterwheel was driven by Welshpool Lock's overflow weir and powered a corn mill. The last surviving pair of the unusual iron gates with their round balance beams, designed for the Montgomery by G.W. Buck, can just be discerned fitted to the top of the lock. They were removed in 1964 and are now preserved at the Waterways Museum at Stoke Bruerne.

Opposite below: With the approval of British Waterways, the full length between the dropped bridges on either side of Welshpool was made navigable by restoring Welshpool Lock. The job was undertaken by volunteers of WRG supervised by Graham Palmer. On 25 March 1973 they are rebuilding the forebay around a 'surplus' new top gate 'found' by the then BW Area Engineer, Brian Haskins.

Above: With the lock restored and the winding hole reopened, the warehouse – probably the best-known building on the canal   was turned into the Powysland Museum and Montgomery Canal Centre. Montgomeryshire Canal Cruises are established on the wharf with the floating Wharfside Restaurant and a trip boat on 14 July 1992. Welshpool Wharf, a new visitor mooring basin, has also been built adjacent to the town's main car park.

Opposite: Using a ceremonial brass windlass, HRH Prince Charles, The Prince of Wales, officially reopens Welshpool Lock during his first visit to the canal on 23 May 1974.

Left: At the south end of Welshpool was another A483 road problem – the dropped Whitehouse Bridge, halting this boat on 14 July 1992.

Below: A similar funding package solution was found to that for Gallowstree Bank Bridge and a new Whitehouse Bridge was built on a slightly different alignment to the original in 1995.

eight

Reopening
to Refail

Further grants towards restoration enabled the waterway to be reopened beyond Welshpool for another four miles, just beyond the village of Berriew and its aqueduct, and on to the next dropped bridge at Refail. All the work was done by British Waterways, who restored four more locks including the next two at Belan. The channel has been slightly realigned here in 1995 as it passes along the Powys Castle estate on the right and the estate's sawmills on the left.

Opposite page: One of the last photographed passages through Belan Locks was that by a canal camping expedition just after the Second World War, organised by an early IWA member, Bill Thistlewaite. They were actually sold a toll ticket by the then LMS Ellesmere office, had the two skiffs carried around the first dry section by horse-drawn cart, and then boated right down to Newtown.

By 26 June 1971 this was the state of Belan Bottom Lock.

Overgrown, with the iron paddle gear rusty and immovable.

The pound between the two Belan Locks was a traditional graveyard of boats. *Copsewood* – a maintenance boat – was dumped here before the First World War and on 29 August 1969 the substantially complete *Berriew* was still here. On the outside of her were the rather lesser remains of George Beck's *Perseverance*. Beck was the last bye-trader – still working after the breach. *Berriew* – SU Fleet No.583, Chester Reg. No.618 – was unique in being the last Shropshire Union flyboat to be built. She never worked as a flyboat, spending a short period as an ordinary trading boat with first skipper Edwin Middle, followed by a T. Rowlands. Then she became part of the local engineering fleet. Father and son Tom and Bill Trevor skippered her and Bill still lived at Belan Lock Cottage when the picture was taken. All the boat remains were removed during the canal's restoration but *Berriew*'s iron knees survive for posterity.

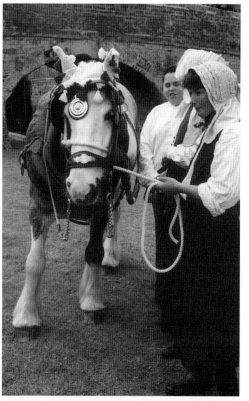

Belan Locks were officially reopened on 11 May 1996 using a British Waterways' maintenance boat drawn by a horse, and carrying VIPs in period dress. Appropriately, the horse was a Welsh one, brought up from the Monmouthshire & Brecon Canal.

Belan Top Lock, like the bottom lock, once had iron gates, fitted in 1823. Now conventionally gated, it lifts boats on to a tranquil and lovely pound, away from the road, past Belan School to Brithdir Lock.

Berriew Lock, also known by boatmen as 'Rectory Lock', is some distance outside the village and was originally restored by British Waterways in 1982 under their remainder waterway obligation to get a dredger through and to keep the water flowing.

Opposite above: Brithdir Lock is at the back of a popular pub on the A483 called The Horseshoes, so is sometimes called after it. A surviving small wooden 'shed', right on the lockside, was a warehouse for the flyboat service. The lock cottage is supposed to date from 1826 and the adjacent lime kilns are now incorporated into the pub garden.

Opposite below: The photographs opposite were taken during restoration in 1995 when this modern addition in the foreground, another off-line nature reserve, was just settling down.

How many boats can you get in a lock? Berriew Lock during one of the Shropshire Union Canal Society's annual Dinghy Dawdles on 2 June 1991. It is an event for portable boats – accompanied by a towpath walk – that has continuously promoted the canal's restoration.

Berriew Long Bridge, No.128, on 28 October 1984, is the nearest – except possibly for the rebuilt Gallowstree Bank Bridge – that the canal has to a tunnel. It was indeed called 'The Tunnel' by the boatmen who also said it was haunted. The cloven hoof mark of the Devil's foot is supposed to be imprinted on one of the bricks of the arch.

Berriew Wharf – built in 1837 – is also some distance from the main village. Its warehouses and office, still surviving on 28 October 1984, are good examples of the 'standard' buildings that the Shropshire Union erected on various wharves. Peate's had part of it as one of their depots.

Berriew Aqueduct, built in 1796-97, is the second largest structure on the canal, spanning the River Rhiew with two 30ft-wide arches flanked by two land arches. Because of leaks, the canal water was carried across by a pipe laid in the channel when this picture was taken in June 1966.

Above: Like all the Montgomery Canal's aqueducts, Berriew has a history of problems. In 1889 it had to be extensively repaired; in fact it was virtually rebuilt and the masonry core clad completely in blue engineering brick.

Opposite: British Waterways again repaired the aqueduct in 1984, removing the offending pipe and making the channel watertight again. The historic nature of the structure has been sensitively conserved, particularly in the use of bull-nose brick edging along the water channel.

Refail, or Efail-fach, Bridge No.129, on the left of the picture, has been dropped flat. This is the current (2003) southern limit of navigation and is likely to be so for some time. The stone wharf on the right served the local Glansevern Estate and also had a dry dock, long since filled in.

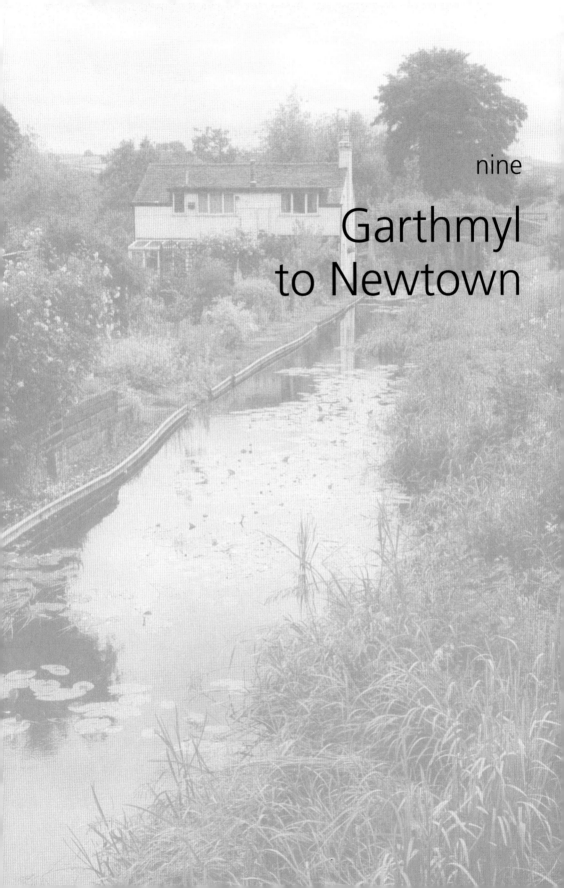

nine

Garthmyl to Newtown

Just beyond Refail is the start of the Montgomeryshire Canal, Western Branch, and Garthmyl is the first small settlement, centred around the Nags Head hotel. Before the First World War – possibly when this postcard was on sale – the landlord was Leo Owen. In addition to the hotel, he ran the post office, the canal wharf and a stud farm. Garthmyl was a fairly important canal centre as it is the junction with the Montgomery road and was a transhipment point for the latter town. The canal passed under the main road, by the bridge where the two figures are standing, behind the wharf buildings on the right, past the front of the hotel, then under a bridge on the Montgomery road.

The old bridge remains, but the A483 has been widened to obliterate the canal, and this is what the flattened bridge on the B4385 Montgomery road now looks like. Garthmyl does demonstrate the complications in restoring this section of waterway, but there is nothing that cannot be solved if the money becomes available.

South of Garthmyl the waterway crosses to the other side of the main road along what the boatmen used to call Finney Straight. It passes through hill farms which now include a secluded holiday cottage complex run by the family of Margaret and Henry Black, waterway enthusiasts and supporters of the restoration. Two more dropped crossings of the A483 follow in quick succession at Fron.

South of Berriew bridge clearances are somewhat tighter. The attractive iron and brick Glanhafren Bridge, No.143, seen on 29 August 1969, was reputed to be the lowest and served as the 'gauging' bridge for the Newtown flyboats. Boats returning empty had to take down their cratches, mast, stands and running planks.

Above and below: Although probably the closest lock to the main road, Brynderwen Lock and its warehouse have survived remarkably well, although some of the paddle gear, in situ in this 29 August 1965 view, went to another well-known canal restoration. The side of the warehouse facing the road still advertises the Shropshire Union Railways & Canal Co.

Above: Although isolated by dropped road bridges, the lock has been restored by volunteer labour and fund-raising by the Shropshire Union Canal Society and was officially reopened by British Waterways board member Janet Lewis-Jones on 16 June 2002.

Right: The next lock, Byles, has been restored by British Waterways and the following derelict Newhouse Lock is the current (2003) restoration project for the Shropshire Union Canal Society. Grants have already been obtained to fund the work. Volunteers have cleared some of the vegetation seen in the picture, to reveal that one of the walls is in a state of collapse. An engineering survey has confirmed this and contractors will have to undertake this part of the work. South of the lock is the hamlet of Aberbechan, which had a wharf next to an aqueduct over the Bechan Brook.

Left: Up to Freestone Lock the canal has been kept in water by the Penarth feeder from the River Severn. The last two miles, from this lock into Newtown, are completely dry and were sold to the Newtown Development Corporation who then transferred or sold much of it on. There were two more locks, Dolfor and Rock. This was the condition of Rock Lock in the mid-1960s.

Below: The canal in water at what is believed to be Rock Bridge, as depicted on a postcard postmarked 29 October 1930. Nothing survives of the large terminal basin in the town and its surrounding industry. The last of the two huge woollen mills, the Cymric, went in 1935. The Cambrian Mill burned down around 1912. All is built over and most features of the basin area have gone, unless you know what you are looking for. The Montgomery Waterway Restoration Trust is, however, campaigning to get the waterway back to a new terminus in Newtown and – with the co-operation of county and local authorities and others – a feasibility study was commissioned in 2003.

One of the outstanding engineering features of the canal in Newtown was the pump, which raised water from the River Severn to feed the section down to Freestone Lock. Built by G.W. Buck at a cost of £1,812, it had a 22ft diameter undershot waterwheel, driving twin bucket pumps, that lifted 80 lockfulls of water 9ft from the Severn every 24 hours,. It had a steam engine with a Cornish boiler as a dry-weather back-up. In 1921 it was kept by Mr Gough, who was over seventy years old. On an icy winter's morning, whilst standing on the wall and oiling the shaft bearing of the waterwheel, he fell into the wheel and was carried around it. His wife missing him, rushed out, and dropped the feeder paddle. He recovered in hospital and lived in retirement by the basin. Mr Gough's replacement was a man called Lindop, whose father was Superintendent Engineer of the Shropshire Union Canal Co. from 1890 to 1922. His brother kindly loaned me these pictures.

Mr Lindop (senior) stands on the wall next to the turning waterwheel and above the complicated double weir arrangement required to provide a head of water in the River Severn to feed the pumps.

A 1930s view showing the canal side elevation of the full complex of buildings housing the pumps and their attendant. The canal doesn't look in too good a condition.

The pump building and the dry bed of the canal in Newtown on 29 August 1965. After the canal was closed there was still a statutory requirement to supply water. Diesel-powered pumps had been installed in 1924 but pumping finished shortly after 1948. The wheel and steam engine had succumbed to the scrap drive during the Second World War. Large sections of the buildings, plus the chimney, were demolished in 1972. The attendant's house remains – somewhat modernised – with part of one of the buildings used as a garage.

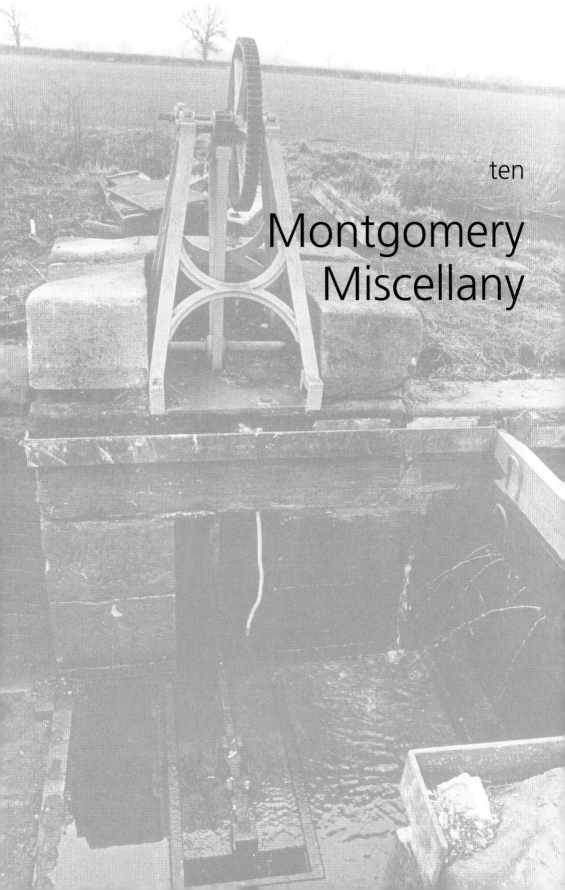

ten

Montgomery
Miscellany

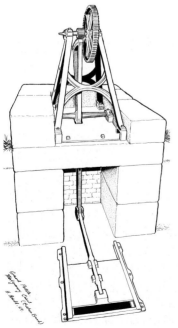

Unique to the original Montgomeryshire
Canal, Eastern Branch, is this cast-iron ground
paddle gear, designed, it is believed, by G.W.
Buck. Apart from its massive construction and
segmental gearing, it is peculiar in that the
paddle moves in the horizontal plane across
the bed of the canal. Most lock paddles work
vertically. Many of the locks on this section
still have it. It could be prone to blocking by
debris and there are apocryphal boatmen's tales
of people being sucked down by the vortex
created if the paddle was drawn too quickly.

Above and below: The last remaining examples of the iron gates of the Montgomery Canal were removed from the top of Welshpool Lock in 1964, for preservation at the Waterways Museum on the Grand Union Canal at Stoke Bruerne in Northamptonshire. With their ground paddle gear (see the top left illustration opposite), they and a boat-weighing machine from the South Wales canals were installed in the old lock chamber. Like the paddle gear, they were also designed by G.W. Buck. Their condition is deteriorating and it is hoped that The Waterways Trust, who now own the museum, might consider their renovation and return for display somewhere on the Montgomery, or at the Boat Museum, Ellesmere Port, which is at least on the Shropshire Union system.

Most canals had mile markers, as it was generally a requirement of their enabling acts for the calculation of tolls. No trace could be found of the original Montgomery Canal mile markers, so in 1981 the Montgomery Waterway Restoration Trust instituted a programme of putting in new mileposts. The cost of the post and a commemorative plaque were financed by donation. The casting was designed by the author, based on the style of those on the Shropshire Union main line. This first one at Frankton was sponsored by the then Chairman of IWA, John Heap, and unveiled by Lord Biffen of Tanat on 10 October 1981 to mark the 'first gating' ceremony.

The latest milepost to be put in – donated by Barbara and John Lower, in memory of John's parents – after installation at Maesbury on 5 April 2003. Cast at Callis Mill on the Rochdale Canal, the post travelled all the way to Maesbury aboard the Lower's boat, with various detours, such as re-crossing the Pennines via the newly restored Huddersfield Narrow Canal.

Above: Once a common sight on all bridges, the normal Shropshire Union Railways & Canal Co. cast-iron weight restriction notice generally specified all heavy vehicles but some, like this, on a bridge near Burgedin, were aimed at the drivers of traction engines.

Right: Marking the limits of their land ownership, the Shropshire Union used these carved boundary stones. Sometimes also made of iron and slate, this is one of a number surrounding Tyddin Basin.

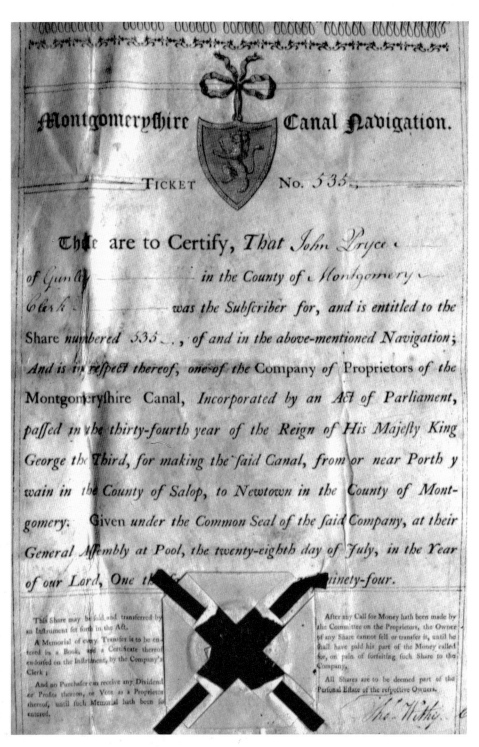

Montgomeryſhire Canal Navigation.

——————TICKET—————————No. *535*——————

Theſe are to Certify, That *John Pryce* of *Gunley* in the County of *Montgomery*, *Clerk* was the Subſcriber for, and is entitled to the Share *numbered 535*, of and in the above-mentioned Navigation; And is in reſpect thereof, one of the Company of Proprietors of the Montgomeryſhire Canal, *Incorporated by an Act of Parliament, paſſed in the thirty-fourth year of the Reign of His Majeſty King George the Third, for making the ſaid Canal, from or near Porth y wain in the County of Salop, to Newtown in the County of Mont-gomery. Given under the Common Seal of the ſaid Company, at their General Aſſembly at Pool, the twenty-eighth day of July, in the Year of our Lord, One thouſand ſeven hundred and ninety-four.*

This Share may be ſold and transferred by an Inſtrument ſet forth in the Act.

A Memorial of every Transfer is to be entered in a Book, and a Certificate thereof endorſed on the Inſtrument, by the Company's Clerk;

And no Purchaſer can receive any Dividend or Profits thereon, or Vote as a Proprietor thereof, until ſuch Memorial hath been ſo entered.

After any Call for Money hath been made by the Committee on the Proprietors, the Owner of any Share cannot ſell or transfer it, until he ſhall have paid his part of the Money called for, on pain of forfeiting ſuch Share to the Company.

All Shares are to be deemed part of the Perſonal Eſtate of the reſpective Owners.

Tho. Withy.

An original Montgomeryshire Canal share certificate with a wax impression of the company seal affixed.